REIKI FOR BEGINNERS

Guided Meditation to Increase Energy, Reduce Stress and Improve Your Health with Reiki Healing

Kate O'Russell

Copyright 2017 by **Kate O'Russell** All rights reserved. No part of this book may be reproduced or transmitted in any form or by any means, electronic or mechanical, including photocopying, recording or by any information storage and retrieval system without written permission of the publisher, except for the inclusion of brief quotations in a review.

The following eBook is reproduced below with the goal of providing information that is as accurate and reliable as possible. Regardless, purchasing this eBook can be seen as consent to the fact that both the publisher and the author of this book are in no way experts on the topics discussed within and that any recommendations or suggestions that are made herein are for entertainment purposes only. Professionals should be consulted as needed prior to undertaking any of the action endorsed herein.

This declaration is deemed fair and valid by both the American Bar Association and the Committee of Publishers Association and is legally binding throughout the United States.

Furthermore, the transmission, duplication or reproduction of any of the following work including specific information will be considered an illegal act irrespective of if it is done electronically or in print. This extends to creating a secondary or tertiary copy of the work or a recorded copy and is only allowed with the express written consent of the Publisher. All additional rights reserved.

The information in the following pages is broadly considered to be a truthful and accurate account of facts, and as such any inattention, use or misuse of the information in question by the reader will render any resulting actions solely under their purview. There are no scenarios in which the publisher or the original author of this work can be in any fashion deemed liable for any hardship or damages that may befall them after undertaking information described herein.

Additionally, the information in the following pages is intended only for informational purposes and should thus be thought of as universal. As befitting its nature, it is presented without assurance regarding its prolonged validity or interim quality. Trademarks that are mentioned are done without written consent and can in no way be considered an endorsement from the trademark holder.

TABLE OF CONTENTS

INTRODUCTION 1

CHAPTER 1: *History of Reiki* 3

CHAPTER 2: *Types of Reiki Healing* 10

CHAPTER 3: *The Power of Reiki* 24

CHAPTER 4: *The Benefits Of Reiki Healing* 27

CHAPTER 5: *Balancing The Chakra Forces* 31

CHAPTER 6: *About Chakras Including The Third Eye* 36

ABOUT THE CHAKRAS 38

CHAPTER 7: *Spiritual Connections* 45

CHAPTER 8: *The Power Of Your Mind – Meditations* 52

CHAPTER 9: *Psychic Awareness* 60

CHAPTER 10: *Divine Presence* 63

CONCLUSION 66

DESCRIPTION 68

INTRODUCTION

Congratulations on downloading this eBook and thank you for doing so.

Welcome to the incredible life-changing world of Reiki Healing! This eBook is written with the intention of giving the reader an insight into the world of Reiki Healing. Reiki is an ancient principle of alternative medicine. It is spiritual, but not based on religion, magic or even the supernatural. As you learn more about this mysterious energy force, you will find it is an amazing healing energy that anyone can use.

In this eBook, you will find beautiful photos, meditation techniques, and information that will help you to use this incredible system. You will learn to let the energy forces of Reiki into your body and mind to heal you of not only mental issues like stress, anger, and depression but also heal your body of everything from a common cold, headache, and flu to major illness like high blood pressure, spine issues, arthritis, and even cancer. You will also learn the history of Reiki way back to when it was created in the early 1900's and how it was used then and now.

The power of Reiki is discussed in Chapter 3 as well as the benefits of this healing phenomenon. Many people are skeptical at first, wondering whether these practices work, but then they read about the healing success stories of people who have actually been cured of both physical and mental illnesses, and they are faced with incontrovertible proof. Finally, you will learn about balancing chakra forces and the third eye.

Thanks again for choosing this eBook! Every effort was made to ensure it is as full of useful information as possible. Please enjoy!

CHAPTER 1:
History of Reiki

The system of Reiki contains a wide variety of different aspects which can be easy to overlook, as they can appear simple to those who don't know what they are seeing. However, these principles can be thought of as the foundation of the system that helps to bring awareness of Reiki to everyday life. These include meditation, regular Reiki practice sessions, embodying the symbols of Reiki, and understanding the true meaning of Reiki as well as how it came to be linked with atonement.

The principles that modern Reiki practices are based on are extremely ancient. The first person to rediscover them in modern times was a Japanese Buddhist monk named Dr. Mikao Usui. While teaching at a University in the late 1800s, Usui was asked by a student how Jesus Christ could have possibly performed the healing miracles that were attributed to him if he were not some type of higher being. This question stuck with Usui, and he eventually set out to answer it once and for all.

Usui's journey took him all around the world before eventually taking him back to the holy Koriyama Mountains in Japan. There he fasted and meditated for 21 days in hopes of reaching a higher state of consciousness that he believed would allow him to tap into the healing power that he was, by this point, certain resided somewhere within himself. On the morning of day 21, Usui started to become frustrated with his quest, as nothing he did appeared to be working. He was just getting ready to call it quits when he was suddenly filled with a supreme spiritual energy that entered his body through the top of his head, filling him with enlightenment as it did so. In addition to enlightenment, the energy also allowed Usui to tap into Reiki Ryhoho, or the ability to heal through touch.

Still reeling from everything he had learned, Usui returned home to his monastery but soon felt the urge to visit a local beggar camp in the slums of Kyoto. He spent the next seven years in the slums treating a wide variety of illnesses with his new-found abilities and helping those who found themselves there to build a better life moving forward. Nevertheless, over time he found that the same people were returning to the area time and time again, regardless of what he did for them. When he asked why this was the case, he found out that they felt it was easier to go on begging than to take responsibility for getting things back on track once and for all.

Usui saw his Reiki as a type of spiritual practice, an opportunity for everyone he helped on their path to awakening their true nature, but he realized that many of the people he helped only saw him as a holistic alternative to more expensive medical treatment. As such, he altered his approach based on what he believed each patient or student needed. Some students would be shown various symbols to chant and meditate on while others might be taught to meditate on specific Reiki principles, and others might be tasked with sharing what they learned with others.

One of these in the last group was Dr. Chujiro Hayashi, a former naval officer and surgeon, who started studying with Usui in May of 1925. Hayashi was one of just 21 students who were tasked with passing on Usui's teachings prior to his death in 1926. After Usui's death, Hayashi opened a Reiki clinic which remained open for nearly 20 years. He also developed his own style of Reiki, which is largely the same as his mentor's. It uses the same lineage and energy pathways and is also the root of many of the more formal aspects of Reiki as it is taught today, including its hand positions and its practices, which are based on science.

Hayashi's clinic soon proved to be extremely popular among the people, and word of it spread throughout all of Japan. This is also the point where many started to see Reiki as the primary path to healing as opposed to true spiritual enlightenment.

One of those who sought out help from the clinic was Hawayo Takata, a woman from Hawaii whose family was Japanese. In the early 1930s, her husband died, and she became quite ill with a disease that doctors proved unable to diagnose. She soon heard of Hayashi's clinic and decided to set out for Japan to see if there was anything to be done for her that wouldn't involve risky early twentieth-century exploratory surgery.

Once in Japan, she began receiving weekly treatments from Hayashi and quickly began to see improvements in both her physical and mental health. She was frankly amazed at the transformation she was seeing and asked Hayashi to teach her his secrets. He agreed, and she studied with him throughout 1936 and 1937, becoming one of just 13 students to whom he ultimately passed his techniques on to.

Takata was the first to bring modern Reiki practices to the west when she returned to Hawaii in 1938 and began to practice the technique herself at her own clinic. At first, she stuck to teaching just the first two levels of Reiki, but by the 1970s she started training other Reiki masters. She used storytelling to pass on the oral traditions of Reiki for more than 40 years. By the time of her death in 1980, she had trained more than 20 Reiki masters, and it is from them that modern Reiki practices have been passed on and codified.

Usui Reiki became the most used and practiced in the world. It is important to know Usui Reiki, as it will make it easier to connect to its energy and ability to plan what's right for your well-being in life. Guidance from Reiki will help to make a difficult situation easier. It can bring an amazing change resulting in more positive results. Its use is available to everyone and not just on one person's intellect or spiritual growth.

There is nothing that is required for you to believe in to use it. Reiki is spiritual and comes from God, but it is not a religion. People find that using its principles, they gain religious experience, and not just learning what it is. It is important to live and promote harmony. Mikao Usui, recommends practicing certain easy ethical beliefs that will spread peace and harmony throughout the world.

When babies are born, they are all created with an abundance of energy. Always adapting, happy, filled with discovering, playing and never tired. As babies grow to adulthood, things change substantially along the way. They start to have worries, fears, and begin feeling tired, and physically and mentally depressed. Adults seem to find themselves angry, jealous, depressed and negative. Why does this happen? We are actually learning not to listen to what our bodies are telling us. We are told early in life to act a certain way and to react a certain way, usually by our parents. Also, other people can influence the way we may react.

All of these factors have a damaging effect on the energy that is given to us by God and the universe, which blocks our path. Reiki healing provides you with energy like it did when you were an infant to help you fight off the negativity in your body and fight diseases, sadness, anger, and depression.

Meaning and Definition of Reiki

From a spiritual perspective, "Rei" can be defined as the creation and progression of the universe, guided by a higher intelligence. Rei is a wisdom that penetrates and spreads into all that is spiritual and living. This wisdom teaches that creation leads to change from the beginning of galaxies to the everyday expansion of life. It is always here to help when we need it and to guide us through life.

The energy that is spiritual is referred to as "Ki", which means the energy that moves in everything that lives. It flows into all that lives such as plants, humans, and animals. If someone has high Ki, they will feel strength, confidence, and ready to challenge what life brings to them. When Ki is low, their weaknesses will consume them and leave them vulnerable to illnesses. Ki is received from breathing deeply, eating healthy food, getting plenty of sunshine and adequate sleep. Meditation and exercise will also increase Ki.

Reiki energy possesses its own intelligence that flows wherever it is needed to create healing conditions. A person's mind is never able to guide it, so it can't be controlled or misused by anyone. It is energy flowing through a person rather than from a physical condition and it is what is responsible for creating good health. If the force is interrupted for some reason, the organs and tissues will be negatively affected, which means low Ki can cause poor health and illnesses.

One of Ki's great attributes is that it reacts to a person's feelings and thoughts. It will flow with strength or can be weak depending on the strength of a person's mind. The more negative thoughts a person has, the more these thoughts are going to disrupt the flow of their Ki. It is estimated that nearly 98% of sickness is caused by a person's mind. A large part of the problem is with a person's unconscious mind because they are not aware of the problem. Therefore, it is much more difficult to solve.

The biggest benefit of Reiki healing is that it knows exactly where to go and what to do because a higher power guides it. When Reiki filters through an unhealthy space, it destroys and cleans any negativity trapped in the unconscious mind and body. This allows Ki to move freely through the body. The unhealthy physical organs and tissues are then properly nourished with Ki and start to flow in a healthy way, driving illness and weakness away from the body.

Reiki is becoming more and more popular because it is a healthy, non-invasive technique. Reiki will continue to be an important healing method as new alternative treatments are discovered.

Think of a beautiful pond with plants and flowers all around it. A simple path leads to the pond where you occasionally go to sit on a bench near the water. Ducks and birds come to swim and feed in the pond. One day you venture down the path to the water and see it is filled with algae and trash. The plants have been mowed haphazardly, and flowers are gone. The wildlife has disappeared, and the smell is horrible. Sadness and grief sets in.

Similarly, this is what happens when you have a healthy person who falls victim to negative energy. The negativity filters in, and over time, it creates unhappiness and an unhealthy way of life. This is like the energy surrounding the lake, which has been disconnected and needs to be revitalized.

CHAPTER 2:
Types of Reiki Healing

There are two types of Reiki Healing: **Hands-on** and **Distant**.

Hands-on healing is where the palms of a healer are three to five inches from your body. There are certain points on a person's body that are called **chakras**. The healer will heal a person at those points on the body. When there are several people in a group having hands-on treatments, it becomes much more powerful.

Using a series of hand techniques, a skilled Reiki healer will infuse this life force energy into any disrupted fields to clear blockage and thereby restore normal function. By researching, studying, and strengthening your own awareness, in combination with Reiki symbols, these powerful principles can be used for self-healing and healing of others.

Distant healing can be performed at any time at any place. Patients don't have to be close to the healer and, indeed, those in need of healing have been known to receive it from practically the other side of the world. All a healer needs is some of your personal information like your name, age, and photograph. This healing process is as effective and powerful as the hands-on healing.

Reiki healing works to provide you with energy to cope with and fight the negativity both inside and outside of your body. Many people have given testimonials about how greatly they have benefited from Reiki healing. Some patients with major illnesses like cancer and AIDS have reportedly been cured using Reiki healing.

The duration of the healing will depend on the severity of the problem. If it is minor, such as a cold with fever or sinus issues, healing will take up to one week, but could take less. If the problem is more severe or chronic such as diabetes, or cancer, then healing could take several weeks or even months.

When a Reiki symbol is used by the practitioner, the symbol will then let the practitioner send their energy through space to where it can do the most good. It can also work with a person directly to clear and heal any blockages that might have formed, regardless of how long they may have existed in the subject. Geographic locations or even communities can also be cleansed all at once by these energy powers.

Over the years, many new Reiki styles have been developed, including other "distance" healing concepts. Then, the idea of applying Reiki to groups of people, places, and situations was developed. These newer Reiki healing principles differ from the original Usui Reiki method for body and mind.

So, if you are referring the original Reiki practice, the maximum number of people for whom one can perform a Reiki session remotely is two at a time, but one at a time is preferred.

To perform distant Reiki sessions, you first need to fill your hands with power using chakras and the Usui symbol of power. Then, apply the Reiki principles on yourself for about fifteen minutes, followed by visualizing the Reiki type that is for distance and that healing symbol while saying the name for a total of three repetitions. You will need to visualize the person you want to send your energy to as well.

It doesn't matter if you are in another part of the world, you can connect with anyone by using distant Reiki to gain direction and clarity in relationships, health, business, and personal issues.

Distant Reiki reconnects you to your inner being so you can accomplish anything with confidence.

Benefits of Distant Reiki are:

- Increases energy
- Decreases feelings of pain and stress
- Increases feelings of love and openness
- Increases ability to gladly take on new challenges
- Improves quality of sleep
- Improves interpersonal communication
- Faster recovery after surgeries or sickness
- Become more in tune with your emotions
- Clears your mind
- Inspires creativity
- Improves weight loss
- Improves fertility
- Increases confidence

- Reduces grief
- Improves the immune system
- Eases sorrow
- Decreases the desire for addictive behavior

By creating your own self-healing path, you are helping yourself and others. Through your spiritual and personal growth, you will advance human consciousness using your own skills and learn to nurture and love yourself and others. You will be stronger, happier, and offer a better healing experience for other people as a result.

Here are some important points for Reiki and self-healing journeys:

In practicing Reiki healing, you must trust yourself and trust that you have the knowledge and the experience as a healer to connect to the divine power of healing and love. Give yourself the necessary time to heal yourself as you help and heal other people. You will feel confident and satisfied that you are able to give healing energy to not only yourself but to others as well.

Meditate every day by using whatever experience you have. The use of meditation to heal yourself is crucial to being able to heal others. Understanding yourself is a guide you will use to seek the divine presence to create the important union you must possess. Make it your goal to understand yourself in all ways to create a happier, more balanced, and healthy life for yourself.

Meditation has been a core part of countless different cultural beliefs since time immemorial. It is a proven way to help a person achieve inner tranquility and peace, exist more fully in the moment, and understand the true connection between the mind, soul, and body. Getting into the swing of it can sound difficult especially if you are unfamiliar with the basics. But the truth is, it is actually easy. The following practices are a great way to start getting in touch with your energy before taking on the responsibility of Reiki energy:

When you first awaken in the morning, before you even open your eyes and get out of bed, take a minute to listen to all the sounds that surround you as you start the day. While doing so, try to block out all of the thoughts that typically swarm into your mind at the start of the day and all the worries and responsibilities that you are going to need to deal with before you can crawl back into bed once more. Making a concentrated effort to silence those thoughts first thing will make it easier to maintain a clear mind throughout the day.

Another good way to get in the habit of regular meditation is to simply become more aware of the way you breathe on a regular basis. As you breathe in, consider just what it is you are doing, focus on taking long, deep, soothing breaths, in and out, in and out. With enough practice, you won't need to think about breathing correctly – it will become something you will just do naturally. What's more, being able to easily focus on it will help you to get your mind back on track if it ends up wandering in the future during other meditative exercises.

While breathing, you are going to want to ensure that you inhale with your diaphragm rather than your chest before letting the breath expand to your lungs. Doing so will help to ensure that you breathe in as deeply as your body is able. It will also help to slow your overall breathing which will reduce your heart rate, naturally reinforcing the idea that you are calming your body as well as your mind.

You are going to want to start with just this small mediation for a time before letting the amount of time you do so at once grow longer and longer. Start with a goal of remaining free from distraction for one minute, then five, ten and so on. The actual length that you practice for in a day isn't as important as the fact that you use the time to clear your mind and become more aware of the connection between your body and your mind.

When you are first starting out, try to meditate for at least five minutes per day, broken up into periods that you can remain fully focused on the moment for. Take some time in the morning to practice, and then again during the mid-afternoon as a counter to the after-lunch slump. Finally, end your day with another meditation session to ensure you are properly relaxed and ready for bed. If you keep at it, you should start to notice an improvement in both body and spirit in just a few weeks. You will likely find that you have more energy, are generally happier, and overall more relaxed.

What to Expect

During a healing session, the practitioner will focus on "chakras" (energy points) and will use a very light touch or hold the patient's hands above the chakras to start the healing process and spiritual cleansing.

The patient may feel some tingling or warming sensations during this healing process. Each person may experience different sensations, and some may not even feel anything.

Reiki involves positive experiences in your physical, emotional and spiritual health. When you leave a session, you will be amazed to discover how relaxed you are, to the point that you may even experience complete tranquility. With practice, you will be able to begin to do Reiki at home for yourself or your family after learning from a qualified healer.

You need to be attuned to Reiki in order to practice the technique on yourself. This can be accomplished by taking a Level-1 course with a Reiki Master.

If you are considering doing "self-Reiki," it is important that you attend a class because there are techniques that are only taught in a class. There you will learn where to tap the healing energy correctly.

It is also important to consider what type of Reiki you are naturally drawn to. There is the Usui Reiki western style, which is probably the most common. It would be very easy to find a teacher for this style. Online Reiki classes are not recommended because Reiki is a hands-on healing art. Reiki can be shared with others by passing on attunements that awaken the energy.

The steps of Reiki attunement are simple to learn but complicated to master.

1. You need to have a quiet place to comfortably sit or lie down. Use a small room or anywhere you will not be interrupted by people or noise. Then practice these steps while following your own breath:
    a. Place your tongue's tip on the roof of your mouth and breathe in slowly through your nose. You will notice the air entering your nose and filling your lungs.
    b. Next, lower your tongue and exhale slowly. Notice the path of your breath when it moves out of your lungs, into your throat and over your tongue.
    c. Repeat these steps three times. If you have difficulty quieting your mind or have other distractions, just take a break. After a little bit just return to your space and begin again. To quiet your mind, just repeat to yourself, "I am

inhaling, one... I am exhaling, two..." Or count your inhalation and exhalation, "1, 2, 3," etc.
2. Practice this breathing technique throughout your day. Think about your breath, concentrating on each inhalation and exhalation, stretch, and notice the sensations of the muscles and skin.

This will develop your sensitivity and help you to become more aware of your environment. This can sometimes be overwhelming. So do not hesitate to take breaks. No one can do this all day, but five minutes a day will be a great goal to start with.

During your sessions, you might notice distress, aches, pain, or even anger. Notice also where these feelings are coming from and listen to your body. When you locate the source of such feelings, you will want to focus all of your energy on removing any related blockages you might find. With practice, you will find that you can feel a physical heat over the blockage when you focus on it. Emotions want to be noticed. This exercise will teach you to develop your energy healing without Reiki.

Reiki Frequency Session Planning

As far as the frequency of Reiki attunements, in general, if you compare it with physical therapy, regular weekly sessions are better than randomly taking a session once in a while – just like visiting a gym once a month won't help you to lose weight. Also, it depends on the Reiki practitioner and their experience if they can go deeper in a single session.

Most clients notice an effect after one session although some need more sessions before they really notice a change in themselves. Fortunately, there is nothing you need to "do" or "prepare for" prior to a session. Just relax and enjoy the healing powers. A good schedule is:

- The first week, plan 3–4 sessions in consecutive days. Then, take a break for a few days.
- The next week, plan 2–3 sessions.
- After that, plan one session per week.

Each session will last for one hour. Typically, most clients don't need to come back after eight sessions.

There are three levels of Reiki healing that can be reached through practice and education. A Reiki Master opens and expands energy channels to people who want to learn this spiritual energy force healing. Some, for their own well-being and others, to become a healing practitioner. Reiki attunement is performed to open and clear blockages to empower the highest abundance of energy to flow into a person's body and mind for the ultimate health and well-being. You must have a total commitment to Reiki to become a Reiki master.

The Reiki degree levels are explained here:

Reiki Level 1

Level 1 Reiki focuses on opening energy forces which gives the practitioner the ability to connect to the universal energy. This energy moves into the top of the person and flows into the mind, down to the heart and finally, moves through the hands.

The goal of level 1 is using self-Reiki, and masters encourage people who want to reach this level, to focus on practicing this energy healing on themselves. They will then learn to work through stumbling blocks they may come upon through practice and repetition. Many masters experience their own physical symptoms of energy in their hands when performing their first attunement, including cooling, heating, or tingling sensations.

Reiki Level 2

This level focuses on practicing Reiki on others, as well as more advanced energy channeling options. Additionally, students will be taught how to receive Reiki symbols and will also learn the attunement for the second level. The Reiki symbols will let the practitioner connect to the universal energy more deeply and learn all that it can provide to patients. This level also includes the basics of distance Reiki, which means sending healing energy to people no matter where they are.

Due to the intense concentration that these sessions require, level two training can take anywhere from a few weeks to a few months depending on the mental fortitude of the student. Students are typically shown the way to the second level of attunement in a single session focusing on an even wider area of the main channel, with special focus placed on using the heart chakra.

Reiki Level 3

Level 3 is normally thought of as the "teacher's level." The Master blending, along with its symbol is received by many, but they are not comfortable in the proper attunement of others. This is why there is a difference between Master and Third Degree.

The Calm Morning Mind (5 minutes).

This meditation is best in the morning. Choose a nice quiet place where you will not be interrupted. Sit with your legs crossed and back straight, while dropping your head and closing your eyes.

Begin by breathing in slowly, taking a full deep breath and then breathing out slowly and completely as well. Use this time to listen to the signals that your body is providing you with, and try to take them all in as fully as possible.

Focus on breathing and where your breath is going.

Relax your shoulders and feel your whole body relaxing as you do.

Your mind is clearing, moving all thoughts of tasks and stress out, thinking only about the breath that is flowing in and out of your body.

Relax your breathing. Keep breathing slowly in and out.

Think of how your breath is beginning to fill all areas of your body. Moving through your veins and muscles and through your mind as well.

Think of your breath as coolness when it enters your body that is warmed by your body as it leaves. Your body is warming this pure, clean breath.

It fills you as you breathe in and leaves a clearer path behind it.

Breathe easier now. Slow, methodical breaths soothe you.

You are calm. Nothing is in your mind but thoughts of fresh, clean, cool air that enters all parts of your body and brings with it inner peace.

Only think about calm, peace and spiritual love.

You are nourishing your body with love.

Only thoughts of happiness and good health are allowed to reside in you.

Your mind is peaceful. This results in a quiet and gentle mind that takes care of you.

Keep the flow of the air moving in and out of your body and mind, filling every empty space.

Completely relax until you have a feeling of weightlessness. A spiritual feeling. A loving feeling.

Nothing is allowed here but peace... calm... love...

Breathe in...

Breathe out...

You feel completely free and now begin to smell that fresh coffee aroma. You are cleansed and ready to take on all of the positive things the day will bring!

CHAPTER 3:
The Power of Reiki

Reiki is one of the most powerful medical alternatives used to effectively boost health and well-being. It has the ability to rebalance body systems to instantly relieve pain and also works as a preventive therapy. This healing process is non-invasive, and its effects are long term. Reiki healing can ease conditions like high blood pressure, headaches, and arthritis just to name a few. During a Reiki session performed by a professional, a patient can have an increased flow of life force from the power of unleashing energy. Reiki's composition represents many new possibilities to come. Reiki healing has been successful for many different health issues, from depression to weight loss, maintaining focus, increasing strength and empowering confidence while at the same time improving healthy bodies.

Call for Peace! (30 Minutes)

Find a comfortable space, dim the lights and light some candles. Lay down if you can, though sitting is fine, and close your eyes.

Clear your mind and think about just breathing in and breathing out, and relax each time as you do so.

Each time you exhale, count down from five to one. Relax more and more with each exhalation. Focus only on your breathing and counting down.

When you reach six complete exhales, you should be completely relaxed and only think about your breath.

Picture yourself walking slowly along a well-kept gravel path.

You can see your feet with each step and hear the soft shuffle of the gravel below. Concentrate on each step you are taking and notice your feet as you walk.

You feel relaxed and optimistic.

As the path stretches out in front of you, you can see the hills far ahead.

It is fall, and the leaves are falling.

Imagine that you can smell the dried and yet still colorful leaves along the path.

Your mind is calm, and your vision is clear.

The rhythm of your walk is soothing. The sound of the gravel is soft. It is only interrupted by the songs of the birds.

They are calling messages to each other. What could they be saying?

Most are small songbirds, and you should imagine they are fluttering by. Picture what they look like, what they smell like and what they sound like. They are getting ready for a long flight, and you are wondering where they will be going.

The air is so fresh and clean, and you are walking, walking, walking. You try to make every step the same and make every sound a rhythm in your mind.

It is cool outside, but you are warm.

You are totally relaxed, and your pace is effortless.

Your arms are moving in silent motion and in sync with your steps.

The path seems an endless journey, turning and moving.

It almost feels as if you are still and the path is moving beneath you – carrying you, protecting you.

Your mind is clear and relaxed, and your body is renewed and filled with energy.

CHAPTER 4:
The Benefits of Reiki Healing

As one of the oldest healing principles being used today, Reiki is also a natural non-invasive system. This healing method uses the flow of energy that balances mind and body. The benefits are felt by not only patients but the healing professionals as well. Reiki is proven to heal emotional and physical issues, resulting in stress reduction for both patient and practitioner. Reiki techniques are used to heal body and mind, as well as the spirit. It has been a proven tool to help those who are suffering major and minor health problems.

Reiki is often used in hospitals as a complementary therapy for patients that are assisted during outpatient care. Reiki is for everyone, including pets. One of the best benefits of Reiki healing is the reduction of stress. It starts in the immune system which then aids in relaxation to provide better sleep, which wraps back around and helps to improve overall health.

Reiki also helps to create harmony and inner peace. It is also very valuable for those searching for spiritual growth. Reiki also promotes a balance of mind and emotions. With enough treatments, people are able to cope with stress and live a calmer and more peaceful life. This balance also increases mental awareness and memory sharpness. Reiki can heal emotional issues and help to eliminate more severe problems. Reiki helps lessen fear, anger, mood swings, anxiety, and fear. It will also work to heal and strengthen relationships.

Reiki is also known to speed up recovery time from surgery by adding an abundance of energy to the patient and ensuring the body is adjusting to medicines used in treatment. It also aids in the reduction of side-effects. It is also known to relieve migraine pain, arthritis and helps with symptoms of fatigue, insomnia, and asthma. Reiki can also improve and maintain both mental and physical balance.

People are constantly on the go. Time moves quickly, and pressures are constant. We feel the need to speed up, in order to fulfill our obligations or to complete jobs on time, which adds to the stress and pressure on our minds. Our bodies, minds, and spirits are moving into high gear. Life demands this and so does everything around us including family, work, bills, and transportation. Our brains run out of energy fuel, and our bodies suffer. It's really important to stop, re-focus within and let your body, mind, and spirit breathe, so you can concentrate on finding your center and calming down.

Working long hours, dealing with emotional issues, and coping with stress are all examples of where Reiki healing can help because of its positive effects. No matter what your issues in life are, Reiki can be the answer to a better, healthier life and happiness.

Reiki is also working alongside modern medicine. It is used in conjunction with other treatments such as medications and chemotherapy, and helps to reduce and relieve the side effects of other drugs that may be required. It makes for an ideal treatment plan for the reduction of chemotherapy side effects. Reiki can treat emotional disturbances as well including conditions like mood disturbing bipolar disorders.

There are still some conflicting research and findings concerning studies that reported this treatment is known to reduce stress, pain, and anxiety, thereby improving symptoms of depression and fatigue. Reiki principles are showing an increase when it comes to being applied as part of a complete overall physical and emotional care of patients for disease treatments, including more conventional care in U.S. hospitals, as well as holistic healthcare centers.

As yoga and meditation have increased in popularity in the U.S., so has the interest in the Indian Science of Life. This science is over 5,000 years old and is known as "Ayurveda," It has to do with using food, herbs, supplements and a healthy lifestyle to promote an increased lifespan. The theory of Ayurveda is that it can help to heal imbalances in energy types in the body that include the principles known as *"Doshas"* which are comprised of the elements of fire, water, air, ether, and earth.

Many things can disturb the balance of energy such as a diet that is unhealthy, stress, relationships, and even the weather. This imbalance often manifests itself as some type of disease.

Ayurveda is just starting to be studied in the western part of the world. Research has mainly been looking at the Ayurvedic program's effectiveness in treating diseases like anxiety, depression, high blood pressure, and Alzheimer's disease as well as other medical issues. This medicine's use should be supervised by a trained holistic practitioner as some could be harmful, especially if improperly used.

Reflexology is when pressure is applied to particular parts of the body, i.e., hands, ears, and feet, to improve health. This system is called, "body mapping." It is a system that connects pressure points to systems and organs in the human body. Some of the studies discovered that reflexology could be helpful to reduce anxiety, pain, and depression as well as to assist in stress relief and relaxation. Claims have been reported stating that reflexology can treat illnesses such as diabetes and arthritis but they have yet to be verified.

CHAPTER 5:
Balancing the Chakra Forces

The recovery of the balanced energy flow of the chakras is known as, "chakra balancing." This is a feeling of increased energy, relaxation, wellness, and healthiness.

In this process of balancing, certain chakras on the body that are known to be particularly powerful points of energy are returned to a balanced state. Each individual chakra is part of a system that works together as a group. They connect with each other, and when they are all in harmony, they end up overflowing with energy.

When working with this system, it is important to connect with each energy chakra, as well as the areas that surround them. The key to a healthy mind and body is opening and balancing the chakras to create a sustainable energy flow, to restore your overall health and well-being.

The chakras are centered on the physical body and can be awakened through a meditation process, or the energy transfer process from another person to yourself. The most common ways to balance your chakras are:

- Meditation (including chakra meditation)
- Exercises focused on connecting the mind and body, i.e., yoga
- Breathing exercises, i.e., pranayama (Hindu yoga)

- Holistically via alternative medicine
- Hands-on via energy healing

Common practices to restore chakra system balance are:

- Reiki healing
- Craniosacral therapy (gentle touch therapy to the cranium joints)
- Pranic healing (energy healing)
- Use of chakra healing stones

The purpose of balancing is to achieve a uniform flow that will continue to provide an overall level of energy. Every day, we are faced with many causes of stress, and demands resulting in energy level changes. Some changes are completely draining, and some are filled with nourishing energy. By managing our energy each day, we can create a more steady overall balance of energy that will then help to contribute to our overall feeling of wellness.

Chakra imbalances caused by demands and stress will create interruptions in our flow of energy. A chakra imbalance can affect:

- The amount of energy flowing through the chakra system, that can cause either balance or imbalance.
- Energy flow, if not maintained at a constant level by the chakras, will become overactive, or imbalanced.
- The energy field will become imbalanced if the chakra positions are moved out of their proper alignment. Balancing establishes sufficient and consistent flow of

the body's energy, and is crucial to long-term health. It will naturally try to regulate and realign where there's distortion or displacement.

As our souls learn and live life in numbered incarnations, we usually learn and unevenly grow which create an imbalance in the soul. Healing occurs when we resolve inner conflicts that create spiritual, mental, and emotional pain. These imbalances and balances in our souls are mirrored in:

- Our feelings and thoughts
- Our emotional well-being and our mental and physical health
- Our chakras' colors, sizes, and shapes
- Things that are challenging for us and things that we find easy
- Things in our life that we have too much of or things we lack
- The many different people in our lives
- The way we feel about the universe
- The world all around us

Our souls will grow in life, and we can seek a higher understanding, health, happiness, balance, and peace along a learning path. All of us are divine souls even if we don't acknowledge our spiritual essence.

By making a promise of understanding, we can help ourselves get rid of our pain and fears so they can truly rise to the surface and be healed once and for all. Some mental attitudes can be changed simply by understanding a known truth concerning ourselves. Other problems might be ingrained so deeply that is hard to be objective about how we really feel about them. Also, a lot of searching of the soul, meditation, determination, reflection, and prayer may be required to invoke positive change, to achieve a resolution of problems. These issues are inevitably released and then are healed slowly but surely.

We are all divinely guided when we are on a journey to heal, but sometimes it takes courage to persevere and get to the heart of the matter in order to face these difficult issues once and for all. Sometimes we think we have dealt with and released these issues, thinking that they are gone for good. However, unexpectedly, they appear right in front of us again. Once we know in our spiritual mind that they are gone; they are gone for good. This is sometimes not a fast solution, but it is the real way to a permanent one.

Power is the highest part of the consciousness of the universe. It is thought also to be a supreme state of enlightenment. After many lifetimes, our bodies learn that inner balance creates happiness and harmony, and imbalance brings suffering and pain. We usually grow unevenly which brings pain and imbalance that tells our consciousness to grow in those areas that have been ignored for years due to fear or laziness. People, events, and situations throughout our life create fears that are deeply ingrained within us, but they present us with opportunities to face them, overcome them, learn and grow from them.

Although in most lifetimes there will be suffering and pain, we can work to overcome them and understand that we are blessed with unlimited amounts of potential for happiness and love. Finding out about ourselves, our relationships with others, and that the universe brings love and wisdom, will all help us get to where we need to be.

Reiki treats the entire body, including the mind, spirit, and emotions. When given a treatment by a Reiki practitioner, the body and mind relax, and the energy begins to flow throughout the body, resulting in a feeling of being lighter and uplifted. It focuses on relaxing the patient and getting in tune with their innermost self. It focuses on letting the world go and bringing in the light of peace and health.

CHAPTER 6:
About Chakras Including the Third Eye

What is chakra?

A Chakra (pronounced "cha"-"kra") is a **center of energy**. The word chakra comes from Sanskrit (a religious language of India), and its name literally means "wheel" because of its vortex of energy. It spins and interacts with many different physiological and neurological systems in the body. Chakras or "energy centers," help to regulate all of the processes from a person's emotions to their organ functions, including the body's immune system.

There are twelve chakras; seven primary and five secondary. These chakras fall into two types of configurations. They are all either located inside of the body, or they are both inside and outside of the body. In modern schools of thought, the primary chakras are located inside of the body while the additional chakras are located on the outside.

It is important to learn and understand each of their individual energies and the connection they have to our universe. This powerful system works to balance our energies. When restoring the power of chakras, it will give you control over your health and well-being.

Since Reiki was rediscovered, its energy flow has been used to effect the way energy moves throughout the body. Reiki was primarily used to concentrate on one energy center that is located in the lower abdomen area, but there are actually three areas in total. The other two are in the upper chest and in the center of the forehead.

Chakra healing originates from a Hindu practice and has also played an important part in Buddhism. The energy healing from chakras involves the focus of energy healing from points in the body, from under the feet to above the head. These points are called "meridians," or energy lines that flow through and outside of the body. They are all points responsible for regulating energy flow.

About the Chakras

Hinduism teaches that the body's natural reservoir of energy automatically pools at several different points throughout the body. Each of these points acts as a type of nexus between the physical body and what is known as the subtle body. Each of the points on the subtle body then interacts directly with one of many different subtle planes of existence. When these all come together, they combine to create the physical world we are more directly familiar with. Each one of these planes connect directly to a different state of consciousness, outside of the one where you likely spend the majority of your time. These states of consciousness include ego, mind, and intelligence which all combine to control the physical body.

In addition, each of the chakras can also be thought of as an energy portal that connects to all the rest through specific Nadi, or energy channels, that run throughout the subtle body. All told, there are seven primary chakras spread throughout the body. They are:

Sahasrara: This chakra is most frequently known as the crown chakra and is primarily associated with a state of pure consciousness wherein both subjects and objects cease to exist in their present form. When your natural energy is extremely high, it can combine with the male Shiva energy that resides in the crown chakra and form a state of meditative consciousness like no other. This state is known as Samadhi, and it is prized above all other meditative states. The crown chakra is frequently represented as a lotus flower with 1,000 differing petals, each a unique color. It can be found at the very top of the head and is often represented by pure whiteness. It is effective when called upon to deal with extreme hardship, things like the death of the mortal body and the search for true enlightenment.

Ajna: More commonly known as the third eye, Ajna is also the "mind's eye" or "inner eye". It is a mystical and cryptic concept of an abstract, invisible eye which gives perception beyond normal sight.

The third eye chakra is located in the center of the forehead between both eyes and oversees the intelligence and psychic power according to Hindu tradition.

Hindu healers referred to this principle as Ajna and it is often symbolized by the OM symbol, with a flower petal on each side. The associated colors are deep blue, indigo and sometimes the color, violet.

The point where it is located is said to be the point where the Nadi Pingala and the Nadi Ida merge with the primary Sushuma Nadi channel, putting to rest the duality of their existence. The main deity associated with this chakra is Ardhanarishvara, a being known to be both male and female. It is often associated with the third eye's ability to see outside the prime material plane and can be invoked when additional guidance and balance are needed or when you need a boost to your intuition.

The third eye chakra controls the pineal gland, eyes, ears, nose, and the skeletal system. It is related to the senses of sight and hearing and has the ability to know and understand in order to form opinions about what is seen and how it exists.

The pineal gland's main role is to secrete a hormone called, "melatonin," which plays a part in regulating sleep patterns, growth, slowing down aging, and also maintaining a stable mind. This pineal gland is sensitive to light, that is the reason the eyes stimulate the pineal gland by releasing the melatonin. It was discovered that the earth's electromagnetic field is responsible for stimulating the gland as well.

The third eye chakra is important to be able to see things clearly and not just physically. Its role is in making you see things clearly, not only physically, but morally and intuitively.

This chakra also plays a role in governing awareness, as well as the way you see and predict things to visualize the desired positive outcomes. This chakra is responsible for the ability to form perceptions about reality. When in balance, this chakra will help you easily and clearly visualize memory and reason. You will begin to trust your judgment and intuitions. An imbalance, however, can cause reality misunderstanding, causing you to rely too much on fate if something negative happens. Trouble in the form of headaches and a feeling of anxiousness, worry, and control issues will result as well. Every one of these is a sign that there is a blocked third eye chakra.

Practice love and tolerance to unblock this chakra. Giving yourself recognition for the things that you accomplish; especially practicing self-love. By focusing positively on all things in your life and how much you have yet to accomplish you will help to rid yourself of many psychological and physical problems.

The practice of meridians and energy flow are the same in both Reiki and Chakra systems, but the fact that there are seven major chakras makes it easier to give specific Reiki treatment for physical health issues.

Vishuddha: More commonly known as the throat chakra, Vishuddha is frequently drawn as a silver crescent suspended inside a white circle and surrounded by blue petals, or possibly a red crescent with 16 upward facing petals instead. Vishuddha promotes lucid dreaming along with the communication and growth that occurs when a group of individuals gets together in order to fully express their feelings and thoughts. It is also frequently described as being one of the primary influences relating to security, spirituality, new ideas, and independence.

Anahata: More frequently referred to as the heart chakra, Anahata is typically represented as a round flower with green petals, called the heartmind, and is said to be the visual expression of humanity's need to be connected to other living things. Inside this flower is a pair of triangles that are positioned in such a way that they form a hexagram that represents the unity between male and female. This chakra is frequently discussed as being connected to the thymus which is a critical part of the immune and endocrine systems. It is generally connected to the colors pink and green along with the more complicated emotions related to personal well-being, tenderness, equilibrium, and unconditional love.

Manipura: This chakra is located between the naval and the solar plexus and is typically presented as a yellow triangle with 5 yellow leaves on each side. It is typically thought of as being associated with a well-functioning immune system and ensuring that the body can easily turn food into energy. It is always associated with the color yellow and is frequently used when it comes to dealing with the transition between strong opinions or emotions as well as feelings of fear, introversion, anxiety or the issues that arise with concerns over using the power of status correctly.

Svadhisthana: This chakra is more commonly known as the sacral chakra and it is located in the middle of the sacrum. It is most commonly associated with the ovaries as well as the testes and is known to help keep the body's sex hormones working properly and ensure the reproductive system functions as it should. It is most often called upon when it comes to dealing with emotions related to emotional desires like intimacy, violence, addiction, and pleasure.

Muladhara: More commonly referred to as the root chakra, Muladhara is most frequently drawn as a lotus with four red petals. It is located near the base of the spine and is connected to the adrenal medulla as well as the gonads. This chakra is commonly associated with security, sexuality, stability, and survival. It is also at this point that the main Nadi separates and moves upward towards the Sahasrara. This is also where the dormant kundalini energy in your body lies in wait, wrapped three and a half times around the first three obstructions that you will need to overcome if you ever hope to have a kundalini awakening.

Chakra healing also helps with spiritual and emotional treatment. Each of the seven chakras closely aligns with mental well-being. A Reiki practitioner can find a blockage or even where one had been if they have studied and are working with the emotional system within chakra healing; then they can apply energy to that area. A practitioner working with Reiki can be a huge benefit to chakra healing systems. Other things that will help include:

- Meditation
- Yoga
- Using chakra healing stones
- Eating foods or spices associated with a specific chakra
- Aromatherapy

If our life energy is balanced or flowing well, it is believed that our mental, emotional, physical, and spiritual well-being will be in a much better condition as a result. Reiki restores the balance of your energy flow if you are going through physical or emotional stress. Even though it is not a substitute for medical attention, it can work along with medical assistance to achieve things that medical science alone cannot. Also, Reiki can be offered to new parents and babies, people suffering from trauma, law enforcement, and individuals with mental health or addiction problems as well as with small and large corporate health programs.

Chakra balancing, opening chakras and using chakra techniques, should be instrumental when it comes to ensuring your well-being and overall health. Many health practices are using these guiding principles as a foundation to health systems and a sustainable flow of energy. These medical practices often begin with old or traditional principles of Eastern spirituality as well as modern healing techniques, that often began with these practices. Today's healing techniques have evolved through the years – thanks to people that come from a large range of energy healing and holistic medical fields. In modern time, healers relate chakras with the endocrine system of the body. This system releases hormones that regulate many actions including growth and development, changes, and functions.

Reiki practitioners each have ways to work with the third eye chakra. The following is one way to work with this process to clear you third eye chakra.

Relax and be comfortable
Let the flow of Reiki begin
Put your hands on your eyes and forehead
Then move in a circular motion.

There are also many other methods to use. A mantra (steady use of repeated soft words or phrases) will aid in healing. The vibration radiating from the mantra will help to open the chakra energy forces. Use of aromatherapy can be helpful, especially mint and jasmine.

CHAPTER 7:
Spiritual Connections

The Rei or God consciousness guides the Reiki healing sessions to create any changes that need to be made in this spiritual process, depending on the receiver's needs. Life holds many opportunities and experiences, some good and some challenging. When you use Reiki as a spiritual path, you will begin to actually see your energy come to life. Thinking, seeing, and doing positive things as well as using meditation to help accomplish goals, remove anger and aggression, as well as sadness and depression, and will allow you to visualize solutions that you may have otherwise missed. This will keep your outlook in a positive frame of mind.

When people are faced with serious illness or disease, they will often tell you that they walk forward, not dwelling on the road they have just traveled. They simply continue to put one foot in front of the other. Negativity will destroy people, they will have defeat in their minds and hearts, and that is a powerful thing. If you believe you can't make it or do it, then you won't.

Reiki not only provides the correct information, but also the right kind of personal energy needed to take the required actions. Our lives are created from effects of all those actions we have taken and decisions we have made in this life and in past ones. Every action has an effect which comes back to us eventually. If we accept the philosophy and the fact that we are responsible for everything we do in life, then we will be centered in our power and be better able to create change in our life that is both positive and long-lasting.

Reiki should be a ritual you perform on a regular schedule, and also spontaneously if you feel the need. If you listen to your breath, your heart, mind and body, you will find the feeling of spiritual wellbeing that you are looking for. When this happens, keep in mind that everyone around you will reap the benefits as well.

People are created in all sizes and shapes, backgrounds, ethnicities, but we are all one family with spiritual souls that can be damaged but healed as well. The key to spiritual wellness is positivity, happiness, and love. Reiki will surround you and your whole entire life with a radiant glow of energy creating love and hope and, as a byproduct, a healthy body and mind as well.

This amazing spiritual path will lead you and connect you to the wisdom and power that is within you. You have always had a plan, you just somehow didn't know what it was before your spiritual connection showed you the way. By healing and releasing everything that is blocking your path, you will be truly healed and filled with everything positive and good, not to mention a magnitude of energy you cannot begin to imagine.

Your true spiritual path is always there, but sometimes, others will try intentionally or unintentionally to make you feel their pain and problems. Some people have negative issues and somehow feel better if everyone has that negativity as well. You do not have to feel their pain and cope with their problems because you have a better plan, a highly powerful spiritual plan that is always there when you need it the most. This is a wonderful part of living with Reiki's energy. Remember, don't let anyone place negativity on your beautiful path. Do what you love to do and cherish what you love. It is powerful, healing, and healthy.

Negativity Eraser – Take 5! (5 minutes)

When you are stressed with limited time, getting the kids off to school, job project scheduling, appointments to set, find five minutes to erase these pressures from your mind. Just for five minutes do a powerful and positive thing for yourself. Stop and "take 5!"

Find a quiet space. Even if you put headphones on to keep the outside world, out. A walk, a park bench, a corner in a coffee shop, a library, a park. Sit and just breathe. Slow, long breaths, in and out. Your mind is full... move negativity out.

In your mind, think of a pen and paper or a chalkboard.

You need to mentally write your stressors down.

With your eyes closed, take deep slow breaths in and out, in and push gently on the back of the air to push it out.

Now in your mind, you can see the chalk in your hand and visualize it moving to the board.

See all of the stress-filled "stuff" in a pile; things are moving from your mind to the top of the pile.

One after another.

Visualize them each going out of the top of your head and floating to the top of a pile. Each item is then written on the board using your hand that is holding the chalk.

You are aware of this, but you are unaware of your hand moving.

You see an eraser that is beginning to remove each stressful item one by one.

Watch them disappear. And with each one that is erased, feel positive energy entering your body.

The stress is gone; school stress is gone; job stress is gone, one right after another, gone!

Still, with rhythmic calming breathing, visualize a clean board.

It doesn't even have a trace of dust on it.

Your mind feels light but strong. The burdens have disappeared.

All you can feel is your calming breath.

Things are just "things." Your mind and body will help you to put "things" in order. "You" are what is most important in the world! You are at a serious health risk if you don't take care of yourself.

Do this simple meditation exercise every day. Only 5 minutes and you will be amazed at the positive outcome that will "erase" the negativity. Soon you will not have anything to erase!

The gift of Reiki is a spiritual one that helps to transform you for the better. When you decide you want to become a Reiki practitioner, you will be connected directly to a powerful, divine energy healing source, and that will be able to flow healing energy through your hands for the rest of your life. This practice is applied to thousands of people all over the globe. Reiki is a completely safe, unbelievably easy and powerful part of giving and receiving healing energy through spiritual interconnectedness.

By using First Degree Reiki, a connection is created for healing energy that will start the flow of powerful energy healing to ourselves and others. This healing process can't be misused or abused as it is similar to a pure filter of the divine healing energy that flows all through the attuned person's hands and onto the patient. Reiki is really an extraordinary gift of the divine that can assist people that are on a spiritual journey in order to bring healing balance to all parts of our spiritual, emotional, mental, and physical bodies.

The more that spiritual and energy healing are applied, the clearer the channels will be and the better you will become at manipulating the energy. Also, we are more balanced and healed when we are channeling ourselves. An awakening self-healing journey will make us better and stronger healers. The path of balance, happiness, and healing has to be cultivated with wisdom and love, and will therefore, align us with the principles from the divine that will allow us to release the pain and fear we have been holding onto, possibly for years. Energy healing also gives us more confidence and self-assurance and awareness of the positive changes around us and in our lives as we become healthier and happier.

For many people, First Degree Reiki is the beginning of a new start in life. It also may be the start of a new spiritual journey of discovery and challenging insight. These journeys have taught others that things will happen to us, but the way that we view others and the life surrounding us are reflections of ourselves. The world is showing us these reflections so we can see ourselves and our pain, fear, wisdom, and love. It makes us see who we are and gives us a knowledge of life that is a part of ourselves, our souls, and our awareness of who we are. Our ability to think clearly brings thoughts of deep healing to us, so we are able to have and live in greater harmony with the universe.

For the people that seek Reiki to pursue its healing powers, it is an emotionally spiritual part of their lives. It is believing that wisdom and spiritual truth is in all the major parts of the universe we live in and also believing that they will ultimately lead to paths that will take you to the same place. For many, Reiki can heighten their spiritual feelings of peace without any negativity because it is a divine thread which connects us and that does not have any attached doctrine. People who feel they are spiritual but not really religious can be connected by the Reiki attunement as a feeling of the divine creation.

A human's soul is amazing and complex in a way that connects the body with the mind. We need to understand that we are rewarded by teachings and healing, and in the end, they free us from pain and fear in order to achieve spiritual healing and lasting growth. This knowledge is very useful to those who want to advance in any way possible. Great faith and an incredibly deep-rooted belief show us that when a person wants or needs to change to a positive emotional state, then the soul will figure out a way to get there.

CHAPTER 8:
The Power of Your Mind – Meditations

Chakra meditation is a meditation consisting of focused balance, wellness, and relaxation techniques that are sent to the chakras. Divine energy is distributed throughout our beautiful world, and also to parts of our organs and glands that are located within our bodies and throughout our bloodstream. This powerful energy is crucial in achieving good health and well-being. Since chakras are related to one another and also closely affect one another, they work to achieve the highest degree of balance.

By awakening your chakras' power, you will be able to restore your control of your health and wellness. Learning to work with energy is a life-changing and satisfying accomplishment.

The impact of programs for stress reduction using meditation shows that meditation greatly helps to reduce life-threatening ailments such as strokes or heart attacks and also the risks associated with coronary artery diseases. The program's results are very impressive, and people involved were able to reduce the risks of heart attacks and strokes by at least fifty percent. Additionally, anger levels were greatly reduced.

Coping with stressful situations is dangerous and destructive and has a very negative effect on the mind and body. Some things you are better off just walking away from or just letting go of, especially if there is no outlook for a change.

Meditation support techniques include breathing, relaxation, visualization, and imagery. When you restore the power of chakra energy, you control your health and wellness.

There shouldn't be any effort from the healer to send direct energy when using Reiki healing methods. This makes sure that the energy uses its own intelligence when guiding itself. After your Reiki session is over, healing energy will begin to flow naturally.

Using the intent to heal, place your hands on anyone or anything. Energy will then flow completely, automatically and always with positive and beneficial effects. Sending and directing energy using concentration through meditation works toward optimal flow. It will then do the work all by itself. Always stay relaxed and apart from this process to allow your message to keep the flow moving in and out all around you. By using Reiki, you can trust it will do its intended work and there isn't anything you can do wrong. You can relax and enjoy the work it does.

The way to heal your mind and body is to allow Reiki to do its work. Silently ask Reiki to flow through your mind and body. You can raise your hands above your head, palms up, and visualize Reiki coming from heaven to heal you. All you need is quiet concentration. Surrendering to allow Reiki to flow through your body is the key to healing.

For hundreds of years, Meditation has worked closely with Reiki to allow the flow of life force energy that will clear any block at any location in your physical or your astral travel. Meditation can balance both hemispheres of your brain which will allow them to work together.

Positive nerve body and brain transformation comes about as a result of deep meditation. Body developing and strengthening exercises also create high levels of deep brain stimulation resulting in maximum performance. Meditation awakens your mind to become more focused and powerful, but also peaceful at the same time. This will increase overall mental health and enhance performance and function.

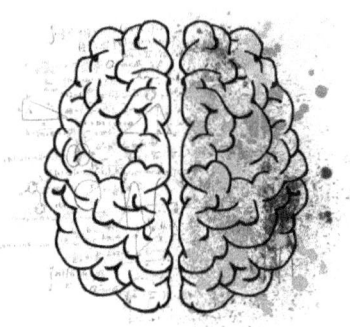

By using this powerful meditation tool, you will notice far fewer thoughts of anxiety and depression and will be more optimistic with happier, positive feelings and thoughts which will just keep accumulating with time. Meditation is responsible for opening your unlimited potential. People who routinely meditate can experience amazing abilities they didn't even know they had.

Meditation will harness the full potential of your left and right brain. This example shows you the traits of each side of your brain.

<u>Left Brain</u>

Has Strong Math Skills   Is Excellent with Details

Is Good with Science   Has Strong Facts Skills

Has Good Reality Skills   Is Objective

Has Mental View   Seeks Logic

Follows Reason   Is a Sequential Follower

Likes Order   Can Make Changes

Is Careful   Is Good at Writing

Is Good at Grammar

Right Brain

Has Potential   Sees the Big Picture

Is Intuitive   Is Philosophical

Can Be Spiritually Inclined   Has Creativity

Is Musically Inclined   Has Imagination

Is Good at Art   Needs Meanings

Appreciates Life   Is Carefree

Sees Visions   Has Emotions

Sees Possibilities

New creative potential is not necessarily genetic. Our brains are actually larger when meditating as we are finding new ways to improve our performance. You can build brain strength and size to become healthy and more creative. You can actually build a better brain by using meditation.

Building your brain takes exercising and workouts for your nervous system. In time, your nervous system maximizes on higher levels, opening new pathways between your brain hemispheres. This new pathway system is called, "brain synchronization," and has the potential of changing your life in countless ways, including strengthening memory and brain power.

Meditation brings balance. As noted above, the left brain is mathematical, logical, and practical, while your right brain is intuitive, creative, and focused. Everyone has a strong dominant side and a weaker side. It is thought or known that people with strong IQs use both brain hemispheres in a holistic way.

Whether you are just learning and looking for that brainpower edge, or you are a person in their senior years with ongoing memory issues, meditation will help to provide an extra mental edge.

Yoga and meditation are supposed to be used to help remove stress and anxiety. Different methods are used by different people, and some have their own way of heading into this powerful thing called Meditation to clear their mind and body.

A Reiki massage will infuse relaxation and peacefulness into the person's very being. It's soothing, healing, and relaxing.

Cleansing Your Soul is a Gift (30 minutes)

Find a comfortable space and place.

Relax, and you might sit in the Lotus position with legs crossed, and arms bent with hands open facing the heavens.

Close your eyes and begin by slowly breathing in and breathing out; taking deep long breaths. Feel your whole body relax and think of nothing but the air that is flowing in and out of your body.

Breathe...in

Breathe...out

Breathe...in

Breathe...out

Continue breathing until you feel your body and mind releasing all thoughts except your breathing pattern. You actually should be able to see the breath that is flowing in and out of your body.

You are now in a different place where your mind is clear, and your body is warm.

You have gentle calming thoughts as you move closer to the warmth.

As you are breathing in, you begin to smell the freshest air. Where is it coming from? As you take each deep breath, you imagine you are standing by the warm water of the ocean.

It is the most beautiful blue you have ever seen. Picture this as you are breathing in and breathing out.

Your feet are bare, and you are standing in warm, clear sand. You can feel each grain of sand on your feet. You are standing still.

As you are breathing in and out, you don't want to move away from that safe, calm, clean space. The picture is so clear and vivid in your mind.

It's like you have been here before. Each breath in takes you to a spiritual space of love and protection.

You are aware that you can return here at any time and you will be the only living being here.

The sky is the same deep blue as the ocean.

Very small waves begin to come closer. You still do not want to move away. The only thing you can hear is the gentle ripple of the water at your feet.

You feel freely grounded, calm and wanting to remain for a while longer. You are aware you can leave at any time, but this space is protection for your mind and your body. You feel protected.

With your eyes closed, you can see and feel everything wonderful.

There is lightness and a feeling of something around you.

You are calm, unafraid and loved by everything protecting and loving you. You have the greatest gift today and every day.

Only the comfort of your true vision and your breathing surrounds you with this light of protection.

It is beckoning you to stay just a little longer. You are in a happy place, a calming space.

You can now faintly feel a brush of the slightest touch against your face and away from you. You can see it is a beautiful white feather that is surrounded by light.

A pure white feather. It is a gift.

You are imagining that you are holding this gift. You will take it with you when you leave. Still feeling the air flowing in and out of your body, it is time.

Your mind is giving a message of "return to this space," that is yours.

CHAPTER 9:
Psychic Awareness

Psychic awareness is understanding the life force within us and the power of the human mind. Everyone has this ability. It is a tuned-in thought process of perceived actions or an intuition of things yet to happen.

Psychic abilities have been reported throughout the world since the beginning of recorded history. Some people claim they have many psychic abilities and others might only recognize having one. The voluntary ability to project your conscious awareness outside of your physical body is called astral projection. The involuntary projection of conscious awareness is called an out-of-body experience (OBE). Astral projection is achieved through meditation. Astral bodies (souls) can move through walls and other solid matter and travel anywhere in the physical or astral world.

Clairvoyance, mind reading, ESP – these talents remain untapped in most individuals. However, people may have some ESP and never realize it. If you've ever had the feeling that someone you know is going to call you and it happens in that instant, or that someone you know is in a crowd and you were just talking about them, you have some degree of clairvoyance to be developed and explored.

Clairvoyance falls into the *sixth sense* category that enables some people to see events in their mind's eye of the past, present, and future. Clairvoyants possess the ability to acquire information by auditory paranormal means. "Clairs" are the main types of psychic abilities and are the way intuitive guidance is received.

In the physical world, information is received by a phone call, text message, or email. The information received is the same no matter which mode of communication they use. This is the same for people with psychic abilities; they can receive messages in many different ways. The four major intuitive abilities are:

1. *Clairvoyance* – (Third eye, psychic vision, psychic eye) This is the least understood but the most well-known of the four major intuitive abilities. The person with this ability is not seeing into the future but has visions that are either sudden or striking psychic visions. The clairvoyant might not understand what they mean or not take them literally. At other times what they envision might be a full premonition. They can actually say they "saw it coming."
2. *Clairsentience* – This ability is about emotions, or physical feelings and those with it can use their gift to receive messages. They can feel the emotions of others. If you have Clairsentience, no matter where you are, you can pick up emotional feelings of people around you. You may feel exhausted being around people who are always negative. It may also be very easy for you to tell if someone is lying or feel the same health issues someone else is feeling. Clairsentients have empathy and are spiritual or intuitive.

3. *Clairaudience* – They possess the ability to receive intuitive messages without using their physical ears for hearing. For instance, they hear messages in their brains that other people can't hear. A little voice that tells them important things. They are highly sensitive people like a psychic or a medium. Spiritual mediums are often clairaudient. They can hear words, names, and phrases from dead people. The medium often hears spirits talking inside their head or even in their own voice. Sometimes they can hear the person's voice even though they have passed away.
4. *Claircognizance* – The ability to know things even though you don't have facts about it. This is "inner knowing." It is simply a person who knows they can't trust doing something but they do it anyway. This is an important extrasensory perception.

The following are Less Common Intuitive Abilities:

Clairalience – The ability to suddenly smell a scent of someone who passed away. A trail of scents, such as cigar, soap, or perfume will fill the air and leave as quickly as it appeared.

Clairgustance – This is the ability to taste without putting food in your mouth. This ability is experienced by mediums when they give a reading. When a medium is giving a reading, they may suddenly have a strange taste in their mouth. If the soul who passed away loved strawberries, the Clairgustance might suddenly taste strawberries.

CHAPTER 10:
Divine Presence

The meaning of Divine presence is the awareness of God either outside or inside of your body. It is recognition of religion, theology and spirituality and the ability of God to be near you or in your presence. This awareness helps dismiss negativity and fear and replaces it with hope, courage, and determination. Being able to see the spirituality of all things allows us to think clearly and create power and love.

There are also people who experience the divine as a risen master. And yet again others may experience the divine as forms of spirit angels or an awareness of star orders in the universe. Some find the divine presence within themselves or as existing in all beings.

Awareness of the divine presence can flow into ordinary objects with statements of divine creative meaning. Locating the divine in others teaches us to cherish life. This is often the platform for healing and well-being. The divine presence broadens consciousness to assist us in connecting with the universe in and around us.

Spiritual paths leading to desired places are energy symbols. The Reiki symbol, for instance, is for mental and emotional clarity. Someone attuned (initiated) to this symbol can use it to achieve a state of positive emotional and mental well-being. Also, after the attunement, a person can use the divine presence symbol to assist in the greater awareness of the divine. When you receive the attunement for the divine presence symbol, you have to find out how it will work for your life. The following can help with the answers:

Draw the symbol above your doors and windows, showing that your home is blessed by the divine.

Trace the symbol on paper or in the air when in meditation or prayer.

Send divine blessings by writing a name on paper, then draw the symbol over the name.

Draw the symbol on the floor or in front of you, then step onto or into the symbol using it as a path or opening into the divine presence.

While standing at the exterior of your home, office, or any other buildings, draw the symbol in your mind over any of the buildings you can see, as an affirmation of blessing and protection.

The Divine Symbol

1. Draw a clockwise circle, starting at the top and going around 2.5 times, ending at the bottom of the circle.
2. Draw a triangle starting at the top and going counter-clockwise at least two times, ending at the center bottom.

3. Draw a larger clockwise circle beginning at the top and going around three times ending at the top.

The divine presence symbol has three very simple parts: a small circle, a triangle, and a large circle. Each person should develop an intuitive sense of what each shape should represent.

The smaller circle on the top of the symbol represents the source. It could be God, Mind, Universe, Love, Goddess or anything the person considers to be divine.

The triangle represents a cone of protection, intention, power, purpose, creativity, sharing, covering, the horn of plenty, giving, shielding, or providing. Its meaning is "connection" between a divine and a receiver. The triangle can also represent a pyramid, which to many people, is a sacred geometric shape.

The larger circle represents the receiver. This could be you, another person, a home, office, or other building. It could be the earth, universe, a womb, an intention of prayer or even a single cell in the body. The circle also represents a community, eternal relationships, sacred space and the wheel.

When you find out what the divine symbol means to you, write it down to express your connection with the symbol. Your understanding of your connection will grow and deepen over time, and you will continue to experience different uses of this divine system as you go.

Conclusion

Thank you for making it through to the end of this book and let's hope it was informative and able to provide you with all of the tools you need to achieve your goals, whatever they may be.

Everything begins with our own health. Whether it is in our personal or career lives, our well-being adds to our everyday outlook and our emotional and physical health. Reiki will add energy to create a more peaceful life, resulting in a happier, more productive life. The more you use the powerful force of Reiki, the more you will feel balanced!

The biggest benefit of Reiki healing treatment is that this treatment increases your energy power to help heal others and yourself quickly. By promoting relaxation, creating a peaceful feeling, and reducing your stress, you will begin to shift yourself forward toward your unique spiritual, mental, and physical balance and experience your own body's healing mechanisms beginning to work more effectively.

Reiki is a non-invasive way to bring positive energy forces that will create mind and body wellness. It is an amazing feeling when this energy surrounds you and flows through your body and mind while you concentrate on wellness. It is a powerful tool that will change and improve your life while inspiring you to change and focus on a healthy body and mind.

Reiki's powerful and mystic force flows in and out of your physical body using crossings known as "chakras," feeding your organs and cells as they make their way through every part of your body and mind to keep you well and healthy.

When this force is interrupted or blocked, the areas that are affected can stop functioning and will be detrimental to your health, which could cause illness or even worse, a devastating disease. Reiki is a powerful way to stop this blockage and help to keep that life force energy working to keep you healthy.

Finally, if you found this book useful in any way, a review on Amazon is always appreciated!

Description

Welcome to the incredible life-changing world of Reiki Healing! Reiki is an ancient principle of alternative medicine. It is spiritual, but not based on religion, magic, or even the supernatural. As you will learn more about this mysterious energy force, you will find it is an amazing life-healing energy that anyone can use.

This book is not only packed with information about Reiki Healing, but you will also find several meditations you can do anywhere, at any time. Meditations to calm your mind and let the energy forces of Reiki into your body and mind to heal you of not only mental issues like stress, anger, and depression, but also will heal your body of everything from a common cold, headache and flu to major illness like high blood pressure, spine issues, arthritis and even cancer.

So, what are you waiting for? Grab your copy now!

www.ingramcontent.com/pod-product-compliance
Lightning Source LLC
Chambersburg PA
CBHW071407070526
44578CB00002B/505